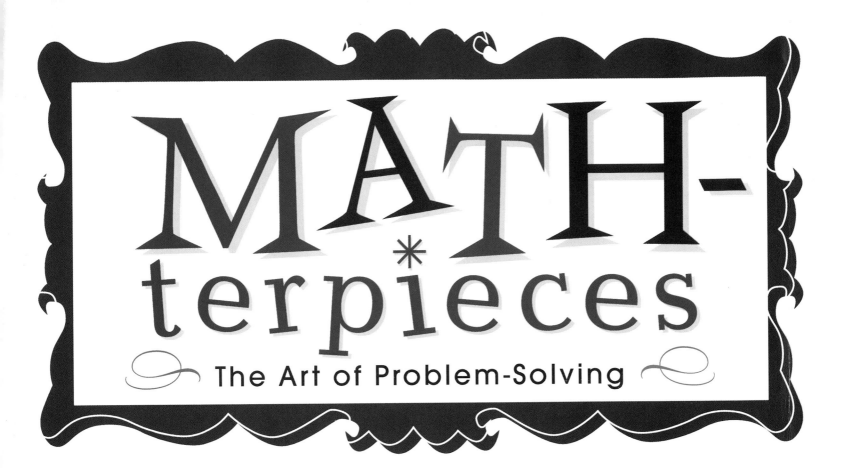

MATH-*terpieces

The Art of Problem-Solving

BY

GREG TANG

illustrated by

GREG PAPROCKI

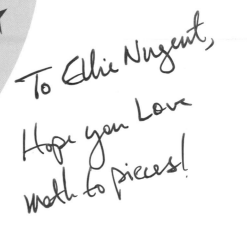

To Ellie Nugent,
Hope you Love
math to pieces!

Greg Tang

Scholastic Press / New York

AUTHOR'S NOTE

Mastering any skill, whether it's music, sports, or math, takes practice — lots of practice. But for kids to enjoy practicing, it has to be challenging and fun. In writing books for children, my goal is to create math problems that teach, challenge, inspire, and entertain — all at the same time!

In this book, I have designed problems that help children ages 5–10 master two important skills. For younger kids, the focus is on addition. I use groupings of objects instead of written numerals to make adding visual and less abstract. Children learn to add two or more groups at a time, which teaches them to think about numbers in pieces, the key to arithmetic. For older kids, the focus is on improving problem-solving skills. The problems are based on combinations and permutations from probability theory, and challenge kids to think strategically. They learn to save time and effort by being systematic in their approach.

For kids of every age, the problems offer an introduction to art history. I have combined math and art with several objectives in mind. The first is to create visually interesting problems. When teaching children, we need to communicate in ways that are engaging and clear. Here, I use famous paintings to add graphical interest and appeal. The second objective is to create a learning environment that stimulates both analytical and creative thinking. Being good in math requires not only good technical skills but also the ability to apply them in innovative ways. Finally, I hope to encourage a lifelong appreciation and love of the arts. Developing happy, well-rounded kids is my ultimate goal.

In writing *Math-terpieces*, I have taken a cue from the masters in trying to think more independently and creatively about teaching math. I hope kids will be challenged by the problems, enlightened by the poems, and inspired by the beauty and diversity of the art. So who said math had to be dull? Enjoy!

Greg Tang

With love to my three favorite artists —

Katie, Emily, and Gregory

— G.T.

You're always in my heart —

Marge and Emil

— G.P.

DANCING SHOES

A ballerina strikes a pose,

another rests her weary toes.

Edgar Degas liked to portray

the varied scenes of a ballet.

Can you make **7** with these **SHOES?**

THREE clever ways earn rave reviews!

IMPRESSIONISM

GOOD IMPRESSION

White Water Lilies
(1900)
••••••••••••••••••
Claude Monet

Claude Monet once grew quite fond

of poplars, haystacks, and a pond.

His little brush strokes colored bright,

captured them in different light.

Try grouping LILIES to make 8,

FOUR smart ways would be just great!

IMPRESSIONISM

APRIL SHOWERS

Pleasant times are never far,

when viewing artwork by Renoir.

In simple moments he'd delight,

a smile makes this day feel bright.

Please group UMBRELLAS to make 9,

FIVE clever ways would be divine!

I M P R E S S I O N I S M

PEACHY KEEN

For Paul Cézanne, still lifes would do,

a cloth, a vase, and peaches, too.

His planes of color, pure and bright,

so smartly capture form and light.

Can you make **10** with bowls of FRUIT?

Find all FIVE ways if you're astute!

STAR POWER

See the nighttime all aglow?

It's the vision of van Gogh!

Bright exploding, swirling stars,

cosmic forces from afar.

Can you group the **STARS** in heaven?

Find **FOUR** ways to make a **7**!

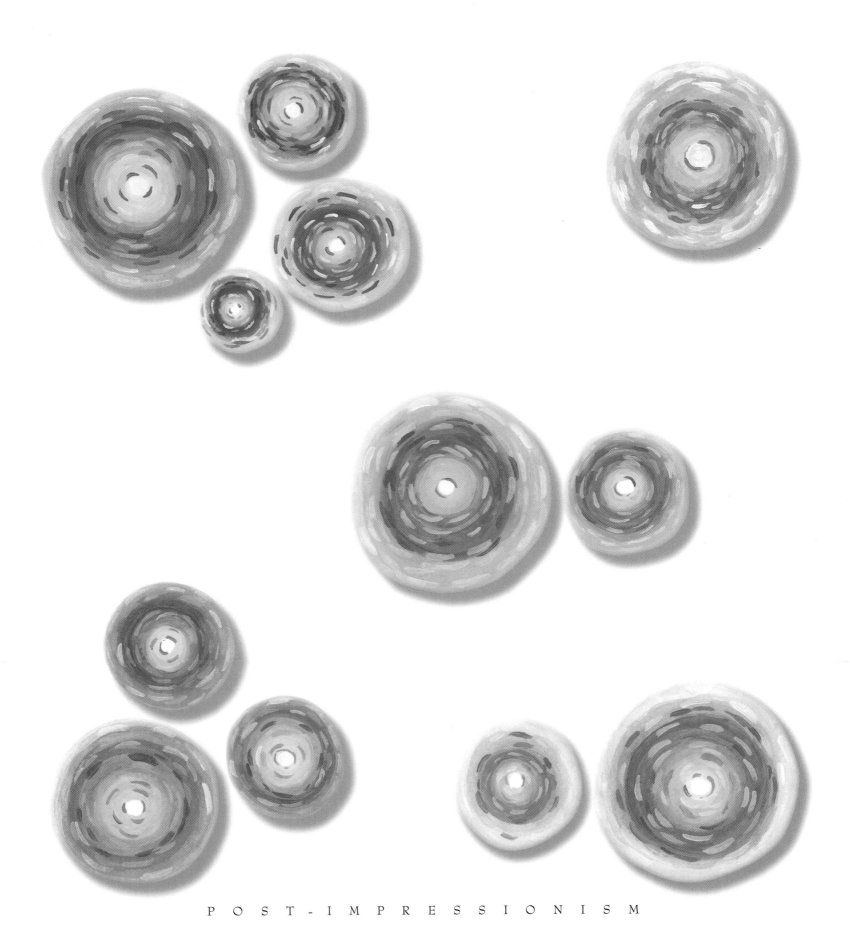

P O S T - I M P R E S S I O N I S M

Sunday Afternoon
on the Island of La
Grande Jatte (1884-86)
....
Georges
Seurat

HOT SPOTS

For pointillism he's well-known,

a style Seurat can call his own.

So many dots when you are near,

stand back and they all disappear!

Can you make **8** with purple SPOTS?

Find SIX smart ways to group the dots!

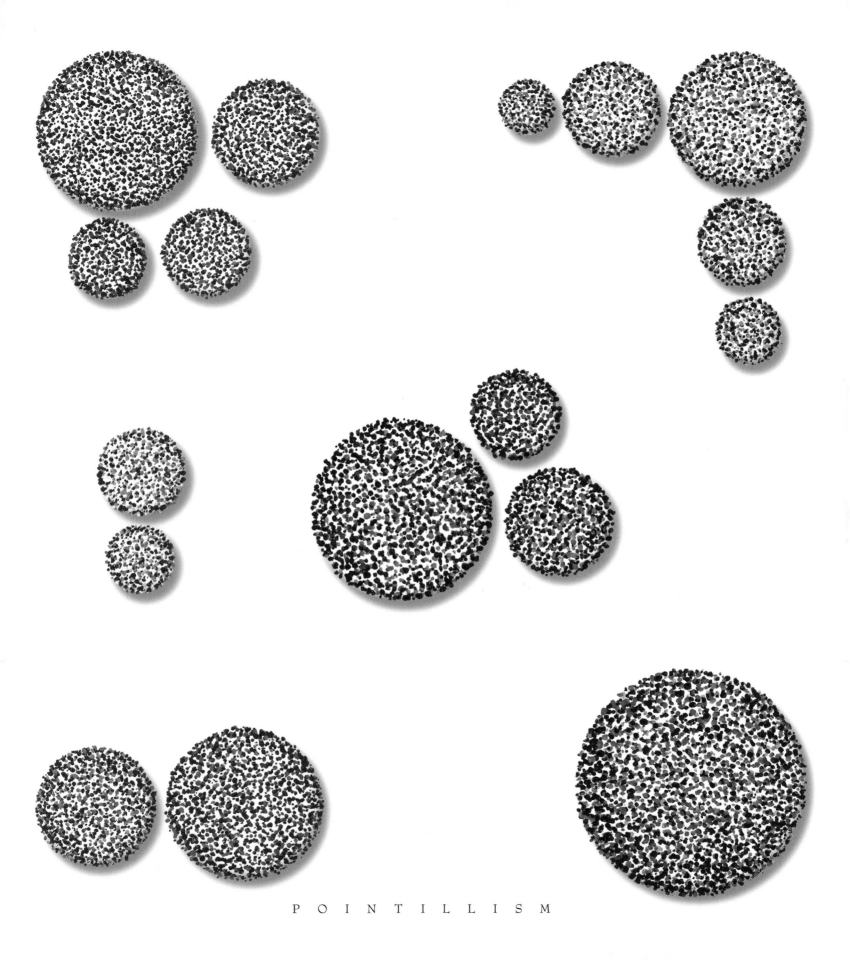

P O I N T I L L I S M

GO FISH

Such vivid colors, pure and bright –

to some it was a shocking sight!

For this they dubbed Henri Matisse

a *fauve*, which means a "wild beast."

Please group the FISH to make a 9,

SIX smart ways would be just fine!

The Goldfish
(ca. 1912)
....
Henri Matisse

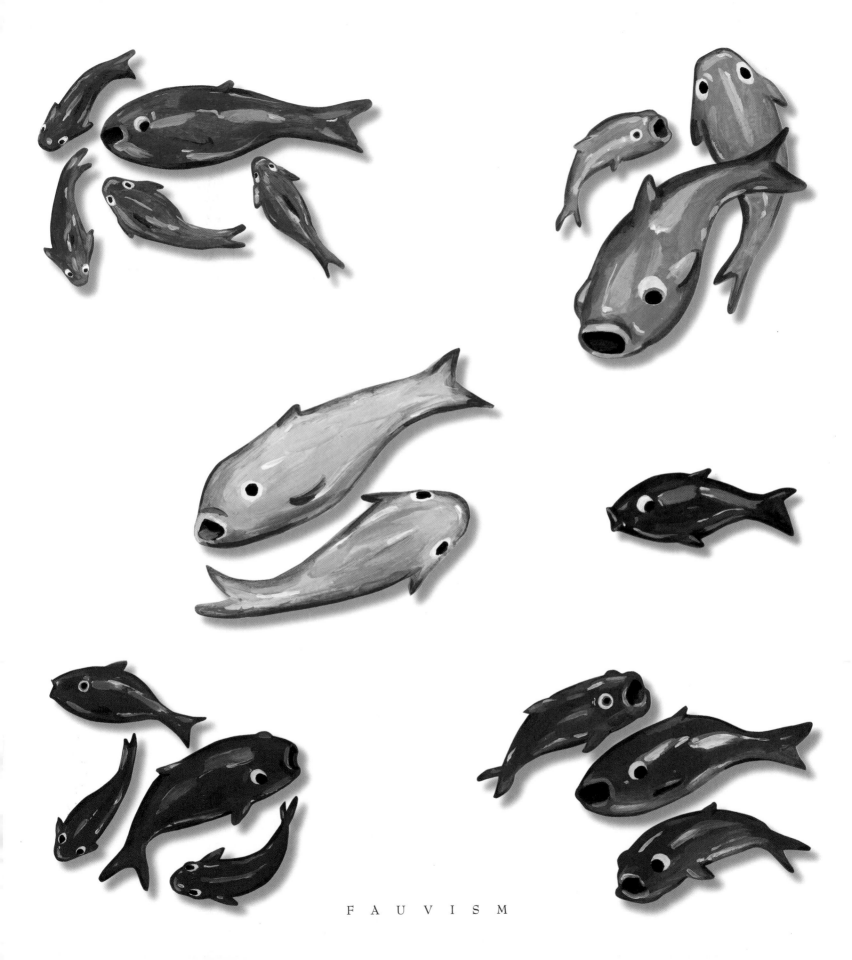

FAUVISM

MIND'S EYE

In a Picasso you might see,

both front and side concurrently!

He changed the way we think of art,

his Cubist style was just the start.

Try grouping EYES to make a 10,

find all SIX ways or look again!

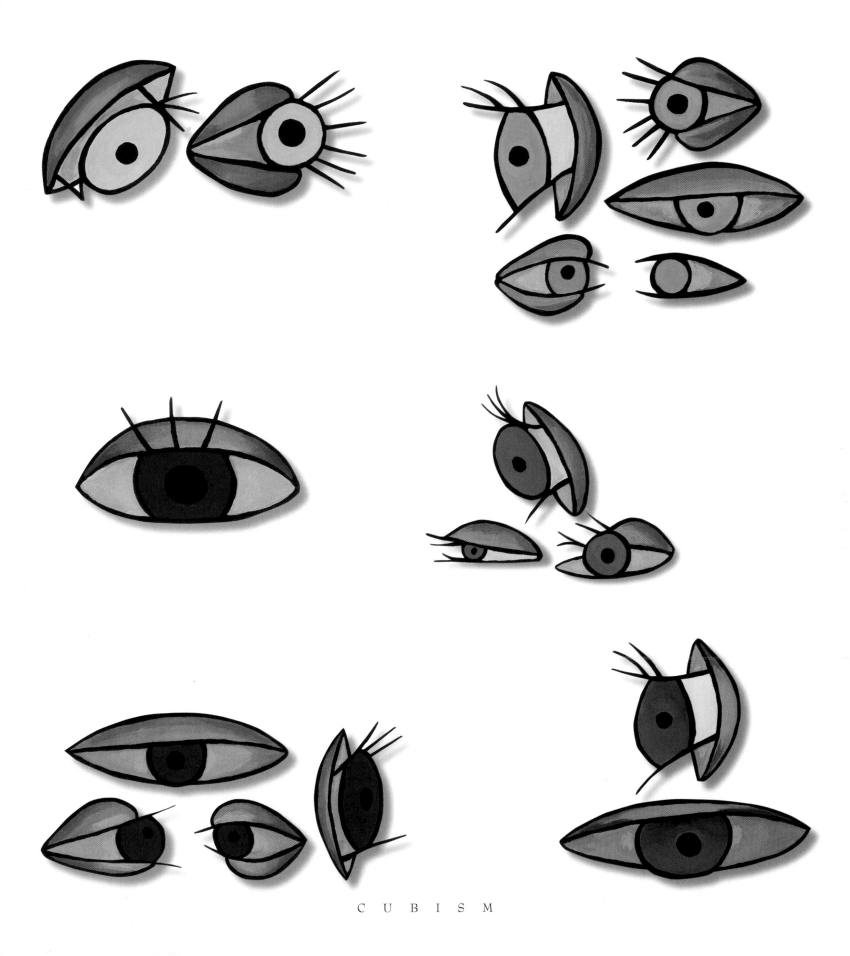

CUBISM

SQUARE DEAL

For Mondrian the art's abstract

    with lines all painted straight and black.

His color choices are so few –

    he paints with yellow, red, and blue.

7's made from SQUARES are great,

    the different groupings number EIGHT!

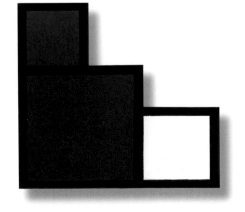
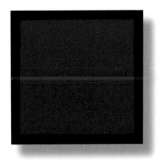

A B S T R A C T I O N

TIME WARP

Is it a dream or is it real?

    It's hard to know when art's surreal.

Dalí's clocks once so precise –

    now they're melting just like ice.

Find SEVEN ways to make an 8,

    group the CLOCKS, it's getting late!

DRIP DRY

A Jackson Pollock makes you think,

did someone spill a jar of ink?

But look again and you may find

beauty of a different kind.

9's are made with all these SPLATTERS,

finding SEVEN is what matters!

Number 1, 1950
(Lavender Mist)

Jackson Pollock

A B S T R A C T   E X P R E S S I O N I S M

SOUP'S UP

Andy Warhol strove to make,

    art for all the masses' sake.

Campbell's, Coke, and Miss Monroe,

    these are some that you may know.

Can you make **10** with cans of SOUP?

    Find all TEN ways to form a group!

Campbell's Soup
Can: Tomato
(1968)
....
Andy Warhol

POP ART

S O L U T I O N S

To solve these problems quickly, we need a strategy that enables us to systematically test and keep track of the many possible combinations of groups. One effective approach is to always begin with the largest group, and then add the remaining groups from largest to smallest. After testing this initial set of combinations, we can eliminate the largest group from future consideration and repeat the process with the next largest group. By proceeding in this manner, it is possible to test all the combinations quickly. Children can benefit greatly by discussing this strategy and others with parents, teachers, siblings and friends.

· · · · · ~~eeee~~ · · ·

D E G A S

Begin with the largest group, in this case 5. Add the remaining groups from largest to smallest. One combination makes 7: (5+2). Eliminate 5 from future consideration.

Now try 4. Add the remaining groups from largest to smallest. Two combinations make 7: (4+3) and (4+2+1). Eliminate 4 from future consideration.

Now try 3. There are no solutions since 3 plus all the remaining groups only totals 6. We do not need to try 2 or 1 since their sums would be smaller.

Answer: (5+2) (4+3) (4+2+1)

M O N E T

Begin with the largest group, in this case 6. Add the remaining groups from largest to smallest. One combination makes 8: (6+2). Eliminate 6 from future consideration.

Now try 5. Add the remaining groups from largest to smallest. Two combinations make 8: (5+3) and (5+2+1). Eliminate 5 from future consideration.

Now try 4. Add the remaining groups from largest to smallest. One combination makes 8: (4+3+1). Eliminate 4 from future consideration.

Now try 3. There are no solutions since 3 plus all the remaining groups only totals 6. We do not need to try 2 or 1 since their sums would be smaller.

Answer: (6+2) (5+3) (5+2+1) (4+3+1)

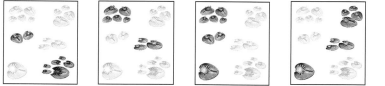

R E N O I R

Begin with the largest group, in this case 6. Add the remaining groups from largest to smallest. Two combinations make 9: (6+3) and (6+2+1). Eliminate 6 from future consideration.

Now try 5. Add the remaining groups from largest to smallest. Two combinations make 9: (5+4) and (5+3+1). Eliminate 5 from future consideration.

Now try 4. Add the remaining groups from largest to smallest. One combination makes 9: (4+3+2). Eliminate 4 from future consideration.

Now try 3. There are no solutions since 3 plus all the remaining groups only totals 6. We do not need to try 2 or 1 since their sums would be smaller.

Answer: (6+3) (6+2+1) (5+4) (5+3+1) (4+3+2)

C É Z A N N E

Begin with the largest group, in this case 6. Add the remaining groups from largest to smallest. Two combinations make 10: (6+4) and (6+3+1). Eliminate 6 from future consideration.

Now try 5. Add the remaining groups from largest to smallest. Two combinations make 10: (5+4+1) and (5+3+2). Eliminate 5 from future consideration.

Now try 4. Add the remaining groups from largest to smallest. One combination makes 10: (4+3+2+1). Eliminate 4 from future consideration.

Now try 3. There are no solutions since 3 plus all the remaining groups only totals 6. We do not need to try 2 or 1 since their sums would be smaller.

Answer: (6+4) (6+3+1) (5+4+1) (5+3+2) (4+3+2+1)

V A N   G O G H

Begin with the largest group, in this case 4. Add the remaining groups from largest to smallest. Three combinations make 7: (4+3), (4+2+1), and a second (4+2+1). Eliminate 4 from future consideration.

Now try 3. Add the remaining groups from largest to smallest. One combination makes 7: (3+2+2). Eliminate 3 from future consideration.

Now try the first 2. There are no solutions since 2 plus all the remaining groups only totals 5. We do not need to try the other 2 or 1 since their sums would be smaller.

Answer: (4+3) (4+2+1) (4+2+1) (3+2+2)

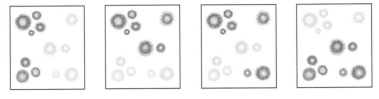

S E U R A T

Begin with the largest group, in this case 5. Add the remaining groups from largest to smallest. Three combinations make 8: (5+3), (5+2+1), and a second (5+2+1). Eliminate 5 from future consideration.

Now try 4. Add the remaining groups from largest to smallest. Two combinations make 8: (4+3+1) and (4+2+2). Eliminate 4 from future consideration.

Now try 3. Add the remaining groups from largest to smallest. One combination makes 8: (3+2+2+1). Eliminate 3 from future consideration.

Now try the first 2. There are no solutions since 2 plus all the remaining groups only totals 5. We do not need to try the other 2 or 1 since their sums would be smaller.

Answer: (5+3) (5+2+1) (5+2+1) (4+3+1) (4+2+2) (3+2+2+1)

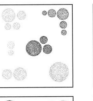

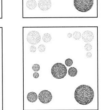

M A T I S S E

Begin with the largest group, in this case 5. Add the remaining groups from largest to smallest. Three combinations make 9: (5+4), (5+3+1), and a second (5+3+1). Eliminate 5 from future consideration.

Now try 4. Add the remaining groups from largest to smallest. Two combinations make 9: (4+3+2) and a second (4+3+2). Eliminate 4 from future consideration.

Now try the first 3. Add the remaining groups from largest to smallest. One combination makes 9: (3+3+2+1). Eliminate the first 3 from future consideration.

Now try the second 3. There are no solutions since 3 plus all the remaining groups only totals 6. We do not need to try 2 or 1 since their sums would be smaller.

Answer: (5+4) (5+3+1) (5+3+1) (4+3+2) (4+3+2) (3+3+2+1)

PICASSO

Begin with the largest group, in this case 5. Add the remaining groups from largest to smallest. Four combinations make 10: (5+4+1), (5+3+2), a second (5+3+2), and (5+2+2+1). Eliminate 5 from future consideration.

Now try 4. Add the remaining groups from largest to smallest. Two combinations make 10: (4+3+2+1) and a second (4+3+2+1). Eliminate 4 from future consideration.

Now try 3. There are no solutions since 3 plus all the remaining groups only totals 8. We do not need to try the 2's or 1 since their sums would be smaller.

Answer: (5+4+1) (5+3+2) (5+3+2) (5+2+2+1) (4+3+2+1) (4+3+2+1)

MONDRIAN

Begin with the largest group, in this case 3. Add the remaining groups from largest to smallest. Five combinations make 7: (3+3+1), a second (3+3+1), (3+2+2), (3+2+1+1), and a second (3+2+1+1). Eliminate the first 3 from future consideration.

Now try the second 3. Add the remaining groups from largest to smallest. Three combinations make 7: (3+2+2), (3+2+1+1), and a second (3+2+1+1). Eliminate the second 3 from future consideration.

Now try the first 2. There are no solutions since 2 plus all the remaining groups only totals 6. We do not need to try the other 2 or 1's since their sums would be the same or smaller.

Answer: (3+3+1) (3+3+1) (3+2+2) (3+2+1+1) (3+2+1+1) (3+2+2) (3+2+1+1)
(3+2+1+1)

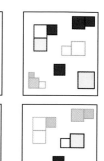

DALÍ

Begin with the largest group, in this case 4. Add the remaining groups from largest to smallest. Three combinations make 8: (4+3+1), a second (4+3+1), and (4+2+2). Eliminate 4 from future consideration.

Now try the first 3. Add the remaining groups from largest to smallest. Three combinations make 8: (3+3+2), a second (3+3+2), and (3+2+2+1). Eliminate the first 3 from future consideration.

Now try the second 3. Add the remaining groups from largest to smallest. One combination makes 8: (3+2+2+1). Eliminate the second 3 from future consideration.

Now try the first 2. There are no solutions since 2 plus all the remaining groups only totals 5. We do not need to try the other 2 or 1 since their sums would be smaller.

Answer: (4+3+1) (4+3+1) (4+2+2) (3+3+2) (3+3+2) (3+2+2+1) (3+2+2+1)

POLLOCK

Begin with the largest group, in this case 4. Add the remaining groups from largest to smallest. Five combinations make 9: (4+3+2), a second (4+3+2), a third (4+3+2), a fourth (4+3+2), and (4+2+2+1). Eliminate 4 from future consideration.

Now try the first 3. Add the remaining groups from largest to smallest. Two combinations make 9: (3+3+2+1) and a second (3+3+2+1). Eliminate the first 3 from future consideration.

Now try the second 3. There are no solutions since 3 plus all the remaining groups only totals 8. We do not need to try the 2's or 1 since their sums would be smaller.

Answer: (4+3+2) (4+3+2) (4+3+2) (4+3+2) (4+2+2+1) (3+3+2+1) (3+3+2+1)

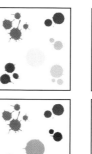
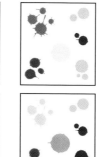
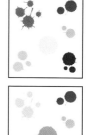

Begin with the largest group, in this case 5. Add the remaining groups from largest to smallest. Four combinations make 10: (5+5), (5+4+1), a second (5+4+1), and (5+3+2). Eliminate the first 5 from future consideration.

Now try the second 5. Add the remaining groups from largest to smallest. Three combinations make 10: (5+4+1), a second (5+4+1), and (5+3+2). Eliminate the second 5 from future consideration.

Now try the first 4. Add the remaining groups from largest to smallest. Two combinations make 10: (4+4+2) and (4+3+2+1). Eliminate the first 4 from future consideration.

Now try the second 4. Add the remaining groups from largest to smallest. One combination makes 10: (4+3+2+1). Eliminate the second 4 from future consideration.

Now try 3. There are no solutions since 3 plus all the remaining groups only totals 6. We do not need to try 2 or 1 since their sums would be smaller.

Answer: (5+5) (5+4+1) (5+4+1) (5+3+2) (5+4+1) (5+4+1) (5+3+2) (4+4+2) (4+3+2+1) (4+3+2+1)

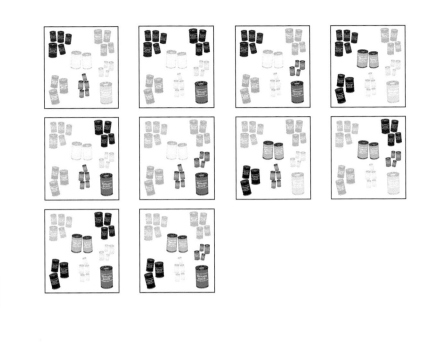

··· ꞏ ∽ᴏᴏᴏᴏ ᴏᴏ ꞏ ···

A R T   N O T E S

Like math and problem solving, the world of art is vast and full of creative inspiration. Following are brief definitions of the styles of art depicted in this book. For more information visit your local bookstore, library, or art museum.

IMPRESSIONISM (ca. 1870): This term refers to the technique of rendering objects with paint strokes and dabs that, as a whole, present a natural result. (p. 4, 6, 8)

POST-IMPRESSIONISM (ca. 1890): The post-impressionists sought to break through what they considered the confines of impressionism, with more emphasis on expressing the emotional content of their work. (p. 10, 12)

POINTILLISM (ca. 1901): In this style, paintings are created with small strokes or dots of color that are practically undetectable from a distance. Seurat is perhaps the most famous of the pointillists. (p. 14)

FAUVISM (ca. 1905): Derived from the French word *fauve*, or "wild animal," this term describes a shocking sense of color, distortion, and experimentation. (p. 16)

CUBISM (ca. 1910): Critics coined this term to describe the fragmented art style characterized by facets, angles, and sharp edges. Picasso is the most famous of the cubists. (p. 18)

ABSTRACTION (ca. 1912): This term applies to a focus on design and combination of elements in a painting as opposed to the shapes of the elements. Mondrian is considered a master of the abstractionists. (p. 20)

SURREALISM (ca. 1924): Describes paintings inspired by or possessing the qualities of a dream. Dalí was one of the most popular surrealists. (p. 22)

ABSTRACT EXPRESSIONISM (ca. 1945): A painting style made up of many different styles and techniques in which artists use unusual, nontraditional means to convey the emotional aspects of their work. (p. 24)

POP ART (ca. 1950s–1960s): Also known as Op Art, the imagery of this genre was inspired mainly by American popular and commercial culture. Warhol is among the most famous artists of this category. (p. 26)

SOURCE: H.W. JANSON, HISTORY OF ART (2ND EDITION), ABRAMS.